D1237804

SCIENCE STARTERS

Electricity

by Rebecca Pettiford

BLASTOFF!
3
READERS

BELLWETHER MEDIA • MINNEAPOLIS, MN

Note to Librarians, Teachers, and Parents:

Blastoff! Readers are carefully developed by literacy experts and combine standards-based content with developmentally appropriate text.

Level 1 provides the most support through repetition of high-frequency words, light text, predictable sentence patterns, and strong visual support.

Level 2 offers early readers a bit more challenge through varied simple sentences, increased text load, and less repetition of high-frequency words.

Level 3 advances early-fluent readers toward fluency through increased text and concept load, less reliance on visuals, longer sentences, and more literary language.

Level 4 builds reading stamina by providing more text per page, increased use of punctuation, greater variation in sentence patterns, and increasingly challenging vocabulary.

Level 5 encourages children to move from "learning to read" to "reading to learn" by providing even more text, varied writing styles, and less familiar topics.

Whichever book is right for your reader, Blastoff! Readers are the perfect books to build confidence and encourage a love of reading that will last a lifetime!

This edition first published in 2019 by Bellwether Media, Inc.

No part of this publication may be reproduced in whole or in part without written permission of the publisher. For information regarding permission, write to Bellwether Media, Inc., Attention: Permissions Department, 6012 Blue Circle Drive, Minnetonka, MN 55343.

Library of Congress Cataloging-in-Publication Data

Names: Pettiford, Rebecca, author.
Title: Electricity / by Rebecca Pettiford.
Description: Minneapolis, MN : Bellwether Media, Inc., 2019. | Series: Blastoff! Readers. Science Starters | Includes bibliographical references and index. | Audience: 5-8. | Audience: K to 3.
Identifiers: LCCN 2017061631 (print) | LCCN 2018009250 (ebook) | ISBN 9781681035383 (ebook) | ISBN 9781626178052 (hardcover ; alk. paper) | ISBN 9781618914613 (pbk. ; alk. paper)
Subjects: LCSH: Electricity–Juvenile literature.
Classification: LCC QC527.2 (ebook) | LCC QC527.2 .P488 2019 (print) | DDC 537–dc23
LC record available at https://lccn.loc.gov/2017061631

Text copyright © 2019 by Bellwether Media, Inc. BLASTOFF! READERS and associated logos are trademarks and/or registered trademarks of Bellwether Media, Inc. SCHOLASTIC, CHILDREN'S PRESS, and associated logos are trademarks and/or registered trademarks of Scholastic Inc., 557 Broadway, New York, NY 10012.

Editor: Christina Leaf   Designer: Josh Brink

Printed in the United States of America, North Mankato, MN

Table of Contents

Think about what you do each day. You turn on lights. You watch TV. These activities use electricity.

4

Electricity is everywhere.
It is in the ground and
air. It is in you!

5

What Is Electricity?

Electricity is a type of **energy**. It makes things work. Electricity begins with tiny **atoms**. They make up everything!

Atoms have three smaller parts. **Protons** and **neutrons** are in the atom's center, or nucleus. **Electrons** move around outside the nucleus.

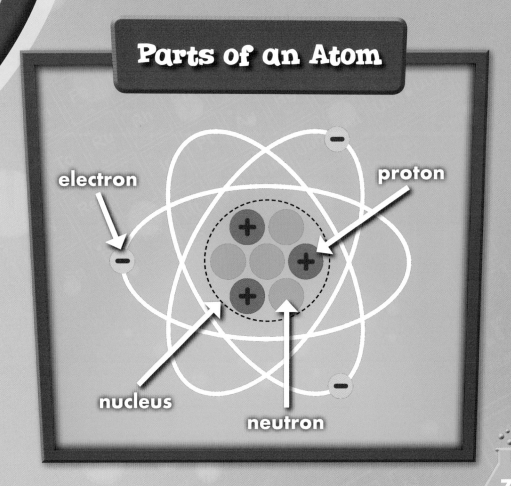

Parts of an Atom

electron

proton

nucleus

neutron

Protons have a positive **charge**. Electrons have a negative charge. The **attraction** between opposite charges keeps electrons moving.

Electricity happens
when electrons
jump from one atom
to another.

Electric Currents

generator

Moving electrons can carry electricity to different places. This is an **electric current**.

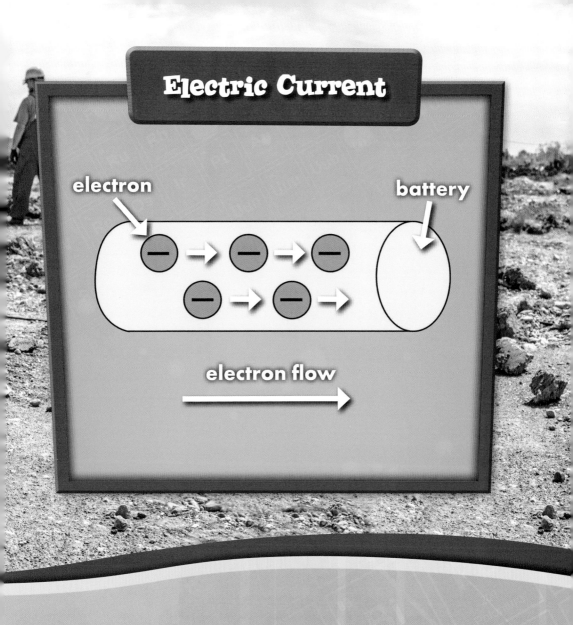

Electric Current

electron

battery

electron flow

A current needs **force** to make it flow. A battery or **generator** supplies the force.

Electric current !
Danger to life !
Only skilled or
instructed persons
may carry out the
operations.

An electric current flows through a
circuit. Many circuits have a switch.
When it is off, it makes a gap in the
circuit. Electrons cannot flow.

When the switch is on, the gap closes. Electricity flows and makes a device work.

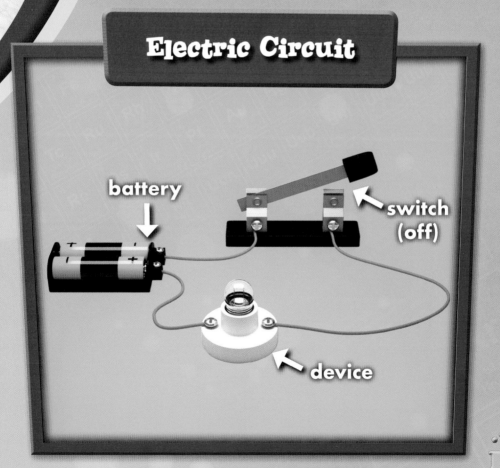

Electric Circuit

battery

switch (off)

device

Electric currents flow easily through metals like copper. **Conductors** like these make good wires.

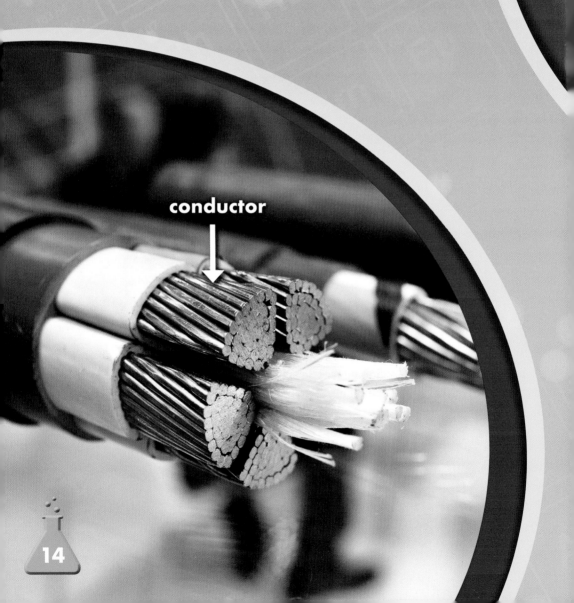

conductor

insulator

Plastic and rubber do not carry currents well. These materials are **insulators**. Wiring is usually covered in plastic. This keeps people safe from electric shock.

Does your hair ever stand up when you remove your hat? This is **static electricity**! The material in your hat rubs against the strands of your hair.

16

They swap electrons. An electric charge builds up. You may get a little shock when it escapes!

Electricity in Our Lives

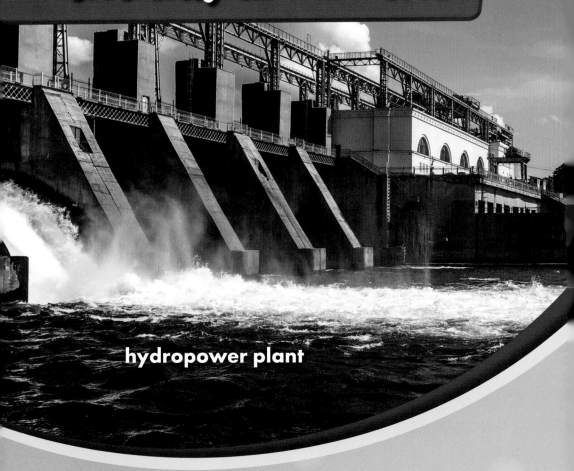

hydropower plant

Power plants usually use coal or natural gas to make electricity. Today, more people are also using water, wind, and the sun. These energy **sources** are cleaner.

Batteries make electricity for things like smartphones and electric cars.

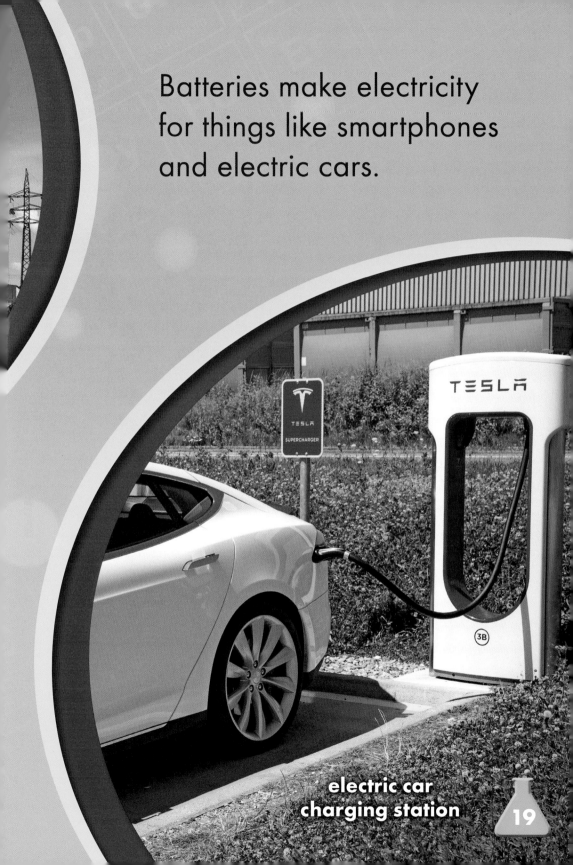

electric car charging station

power lines

Power lines carry electricity from power plants to homes. We use electricity to cook, heat homes, run refrigerators, and more. Life is easier with electricity!

Bend Water

See static electricity in action with this easy activity!

What you will need:
- a dry plastic comb
- a working faucet
- a head of clean hair

---

1. Turn the faucet on low. The stream of flowing water should be thin.
2. Take the comb and pull it through your hair ten times.
3. Slowly bring the comb close to the flowing water. Do not touch the water. The water should bend towards the comb!

What happened?

Electrons from your hair gathered on the comb. This gave the comb a negative charge. Things with a negative charge attract things with a positive charge, like water. The comb pulls the water toward it!

Glossary

atoms—units of one of the basic substances that make up the planet; atoms make up everything in the universe.

attraction—a force that pulls something toward something else

charge—the amount of positive or negative electricity

circuit—the closed circular path of an electric current

conductors—materials that electricity can flow through

electric current—the flow of electricity

electrons—the parts of an atom that have a negative charge

energy—useable power that allows things to be active

force—strength or power

generator—something that creates electric energy

insulators—materials that electricity cannot flow through

neutrons—the parts of an atom that have no charge

protons—the parts of an atom that have a positive charge

sources—where things start or come from

static electricity—electricity that builds up in one place

To Learn More

AT THE LIBRARY
Byrne, Eileen. *Electricity for the Future*. New York, N.Y.: Gareth Stevens Publishing, 2013.

Polinsky, Paige V. *Super Simple Experiments With Electricity: Fun and Innovative Science Projects*. Minneapolis, Minn.: Super Sandcastle, 2017.

Slade, Suzanne. *Zap!: Wile E. Coyote Experiments with Energy*. North Mankato, Minn.: Capstone Press, 2014.

ON THE WEB
Learning more about electricity is as easy as 1, 2, 3.

1. Go to www.factsurfer.com.

2. Enter "electricity" into the search box.

3. Click the "Surf" button and you will see a list of related web sites.

With factsurfer.com, finding more information is just a click away.

Index

The images in this book are reproduced through the courtesy of: charobnica, front cover (periodic table); John Dakapu, front cover (circuit); Ase, front cover (electricity); Sebestyen Balint, front cover (hero); OJO Images, p. 4; Smelov, p. 5; Wavebreakmedia, p. 6; ShadeDesign, p. 7; Dark Moon Pictures, p. 8; Triff, p. 9; Roman023_photography, pp. 10-11; papi8888, p. 12; haryigit, p. 13; Sergey Ryzhov, p. 14; PavelRodimov, p. 15; Richardwlh, p. 16; alexis84, p. 17; Maxim Burkovskiy, p. 18; Fedor Selivanov, p. 19; QiuJu Song, p. 20; Tamara JM Peterson, p. 21; kyoshino, p. 24.